Blockchain for Beginners

A Simple Guide to Understanding the Technology Behind Cryptocurrencies

Roman F. Preciado

Table of Contents

SECTION 4: The Basics of Cryptocurrency Technology

SECTION 5: The Blockchain and Cryptocurrency Ecosystem

- Who are the Key Players and Stakeholders in the Blockchain and Cryptocurrency Ecosystem?
- What are the Main Platforms and Applications of Blockchain and Cryptocurrency?
- What are the Main Trends and Developments in the Blockchain and Cryptocurrency Ecosystem?
- What are the Main Issues and Debates in the Blockchain and Cryptocurrency Ecosystem?

Chapter 6: The Future of Blockchain and Cryptocurrency

- What are the Potential Impacts and Implications of Blockchain and Cryptocurrency for Society, Economy, and Environment?

- What are the Emerging and Innovative Use Cases and Opportunities of Blockchain and Cryptocurrency?
- What are the Risks and Challenges of Blockchain and Cryptocurrency for Security, Privacy, and Regulation?
- What are the Best Practices and Recommendations for Blockchain and Cryptocurrency Users, Investors, and Developers?

Conclusion

Acknowledgment

SECTION 1

Introduction

Blockchain and cryptocurrency are two of the most popular and influential topics in the world of technology, finance, and innovation. They have been hailed as revolutionary and disruptive forces that can transform the way we exchange value, store data, and coordinate actions across the globe. They have also been criticized as risky and unstable phenomena that can undermine the security, privacy, and regulation of existing systems and institutions.

Whether you are a supporter or a skeptic of blockchain and cryptocurrency, you cannot ignore their impact and potential for the future.

But what exactly are blockchain and cryptocurrency? How do they work, and why do they matter? How can you use, invest, and benefit from them? And what are the challenges and opportunities that they pose for society, economy, and environment? These are some of the questions that this book will try to answer, in a simple and accessible way, for beginners who want to understand the technology behind cryptocurrencies.

In this section, we will introduce the basic concepts and definitions of blockchain and cryptocurrency, and explain why they are important and relevant for the modern world. We will also give an overview of how this book is organized, and what you can expect to learn from it.

What is Blockchain?

Blockchain is a technology that allows data to be stored and transferred in a decentralized, distributed, and secure way. It is essentially a system of records, or a ledger, that is shared and maintained by a network of computers, or nodes, without the need for a central authority, intermediary, or trust. Each record, or block, contains information about a transaction, such as the sender, the receiver, the amount, the date, and the time. Each block also contains a cryptographic hash, or a unique code, that links it to the previous block, forming a chain of blocks. This chain of blocks, or blockchain, is constantly updated and verified by the network, using a consensus mechanism, or a set of rules, that ensures that all nodes agree on the validity and order of the blocks. Once a block is added to the blockchain, it cannot be altered or deleted, making the blockchain immutable, transparent, and verifiable.

Blockchain technology has many applications and advantages, such as:

- It enables peer-to-peer transactions, without the need for intermediaries, such as banks, brokers, or agents, reducing costs, delays, and risks.

- It provides a secure and reliable way of storing and transferring data, without the risk of corruption, tampering, or hacking, by using encryption, hashing, and digital signatures.

- It creates a transparent and accountable system of records that can be accessed and audited by anyone, at any time, enhancing trust and cooperation among participants.

- It supports a variety of data types, such as currency, assets, contracts, identity, votes, and more, enabling the creation of new and innovative services and solutions.

Blockchain technology is not a single or uniform technology, but rather a family of technologies that can vary in terms of design, architecture, functionality, and performance. Some of the main types and components of blockchain technology are:

- **Public vs private blockchains:** A public blockchain is open and accessible to anyone, who can join the network, view the blockchain, and participate in the transactions. A private blockchain is closed and restricted to a specific group of participants, who have the permission to access the blockchain and perform the transactions.

- **Permissionless vs permissioned blockchains:** A permissionless blockchain is a type of public blockchain, where anyone can join the network, without the need for authorization or identification. A permissioned blockchain is a type of private blockchain, where participants need to be authorized and identified by a central entity, or a consortium of entities, to join the network and perform the transactions.

- **Proof-of-work vs proof-of-stake blockchains:** Proof-of-work and proof-of-stake are two of the most common consensus mechanisms, or rules, that are used to validate and update the blocks on the blockchain. Proof-of-work requires the nodes to compete and solve a complex mathematical puzzle, using a lot of computational power and energy, to create and add a new block to the blockchain. Proof-of-stake requires the nodes to stake, or lock, a certain amount of their own tokens, or digital assets, to create and add a new block to the blockchain, based on their stake and reputation.

What is Cryptocurrency?

Cryptocurrency is a type of digital currency that is created and exchanged using blockchain technology. It is a medium of exchange that can be used to buy, sell, or trade goods and services, online or offline, without the need for a central authority, intermediary, or trust. It is also a store of value that can be used to save, invest, or speculate, depending on the market conditions and the user's preferences. It is also a unit of account that can be used to measure and compare the value of different goods and services, across different platforms and markets.

Cryptocurrency has many features and benefits, such as:

- It is decentralized and distributed, meaning that it is not controlled or issued by any single entity, such as a government, a bank, or a corporation, but rather by the network of users, who collectively manage and maintain the cryptocurrency system.

- It is secure and anonymous, meaning that it uses encryption, hashing, and digital signatures, to protect the transactions and the identities of the users, from fraud, theft, or censorship.

- It is fast and cheap, meaning that it can process and confirm transactions in a matter of minutes, or even seconds, with minimal or no fees, compared to traditional payment systems, that can take days, or even weeks, and charge high fees.

- It is scarce and divisible, meaning that it has a limited and fixed supply, that cannot be inflated or manipulated, and that it can be divided into smaller units, or fractions, to facilitate microtransactions and payments.

Cryptocurrency is not a single or uniform currency, but rather a family of currencies that can vary in terms of design, functionality, and performance. Some of the main types and components of cryptocurrency are:

- **Bitcoin vs altcoins:** Bitcoin is the first and the most popular cryptocurrency, that was created in 2009, by an anonymous person or group, known as Satoshi Nakamoto. It is based on a public, permissionless, and proof-of-work blockchain that has a maximum supply of 21 million bitcoins. Altcoins are alternative cryptocurrencies that were created after Bitcoin, either by modifying or improving some aspects of Bitcoin, or by creating a completely new and different cryptocurrency. There are thousands of altcoins, such as Ethereum, Litecoin, Ripple, and more, each with its own features and advantages.

- **Tokens vs coins:** Tokens and coins are two types of digital assets that can be created and exchanged using blockchain technology. Coins are native to their own blockchain, and can be used as a currency, or a fuel, to power the blockchain. Tokens are created on top of an existing blockchain, and can represent a variety of things, such as assets, rights, services, or utilities. Tokens can be classified into different categories, such as utility tokens, security tokens, governance tokens, and more, depending on their purpose and function.

- **Stablecoins vs volatile coins:** Stablecoins and volatile coins are two types of cryptocurrencies that differ in terms of their price stability and volatility. Stablecoins are cryptocurrencies that are pegged, or linked, to a stable asset, such as a fiat currency, a commodity, or a basket of assets, to maintain a stable and predictable value. Volatile coins are cryptocurrencies that are not pegged, or linked, to any stable asset, and that can experience significant and unpredictable fluctuations in their value, depending on the market forces of supply and demand.

Why Blockchain and Cryptocurrency Matter?

Blockchain and cryptocurrency matter because they have the potential to change the world, for better or for worse, depending on how they are used and regulated. They can offer new and innovative solutions and opportunities, for various sectors and domains, such as:

- **Finance:** Blockchain and cryptocurrency can enable faster, cheaper, and more inclusive financial services and products, such as payments, remittances, lending, saving, investing, and more, especially for the unbanked and underbanked populations, who lack access to traditional financial institutions and systems.

- **Business:** Blockchain and cryptocurrency can enable more efficient, transparent, and secure business processes and transactions, such as supply chain management, trade finance, asset tokenization, smart contracts, and more, especially for the small and medium enterprises, who face high costs and barriers to entry and expansion.

- **Governance:** Blockchain and cryptocurrency can enable more democratic, participatory, and accountable governance systems and mechanisms, such as voting, identity, reputation, consensus, and more, especially for the marginalized and oppressed communities, who suffer from corruption, discrimination, and injustice.

- **Society:** Blockchain and cryptocurrency can enable more social, cultural, and environmental impact and value creation, such as philanthropy, crowdfunding, social media, content creation, and more, especially for the creative and altruistic individuals and groups, who want to make a difference and contribute to the common good.

However, blockchain and cryptocurrency also pose significant challenges and risks, for various sectors and domains, such as:

- **Security:** Blockchain and cryptocurrency can be vulnerable to cyberattacks, hacks, thefts, and frauds, that can compromise the integrity, availability, and confidentiality of the data and the assets, especially for the inexperienced and unaware users, who lack the necessary knowledge and skills to protect themselves and their resources.

- **Privacy:** Blockchain and cryptocurrency can be invasive, intrusive, and exploitative, that can expose the personal and sensitive information and activities of the users, especially for the public and permissionless blockchains, where the transactions and the identities are visible and traceable by anyone, at any time.

- **Regulation:** Blockchain and cryptocurrency can be illegal, unethical, and harmful, that can violate the laws, norms, and values of the existing systems and institutions, especially for the governments, regulators, and authorities, who face difficulties and dilemmas in overseeing and controlling the blockchain and cryptocurrency activities and actors.

- **Education:** Blockchain and cryptocurrency can be complex, confusing, and overwhelming, that can create a knowledge and skills gap and barrier for the users, especially for the beginners, who lack the necessary resources and guidance to understand and use the blockchain and cryptocurrency technology and tools.

Therefore, blockchain and cryptocurrency are not only technical, but also social, economic, and political phenomena that have both positive and negative impacts and implications for the world. They require a balanced and holistic approach, that considers the opportunities and challenges, the benefits and risks, and the advantages and disadvantages, of these emerging and evolving technologies.

How This Book is Organized?

This book is organized into six chapters, each covering a different aspect and perspective of blockchain and cryptocurrency, for beginners who want to understand the technology behind cryptocurrencies. The chapters are as follows:

- **Section 1:** Introduction: This chapter introduces the basic concepts and definitions of blockchain and cryptocurrency, and explains why they are important and relevant for the modern world. It also gives an overview of how this book is organized, and what you can expect to learn from it.

- **Section 2:** The History and Evolution of Blockchain and Cryptocurrency: This chapter traces the origins and development of blockchain and cryptocurrency, from the creation of Bitcoin, to the rise and fall of the first wave of cryptocurrencies, to the emergence and growth of the second wave of cryptocurrencies, to the challenges and opportunities of the third wave of cryptocurrencies.

- **Section 3:** The Basics of Blockchain Technology: This chapter explains the core principles and mechanisms of blockchain technology, such as how it works, what are its key features and benefits, what are its main types and components, and what are its common challenges and limitations.

- **Section 4:** The Basics of Cryptocurrency Technology: This chapter explains the core principles and mechanisms of cryptocurrency technology, such as how it works, what are its key features and benefits, what are its main types and components, and what are its common challenges and limitations.

- **Section 5:** The Blockchain and Cryptocurrency Ecosystem: This chapter describes the main actors and stakeholders, platforms and applications, trends and developments, and issues and debates, in the blockchain and cryptocurrency ecosystem, and how they interact and influence each other.

- **Section 6:** The Future of Blockchain and Cryptocurrency: This chapter explores the potential impacts and implications, use cases and opportunities, risks and challenges, and best practices and recommendations, of blockchain and cryptocurrency, for society, economy, and environment, and for the users, investors, and developers.

By the end of this book, you will have a solid and comprehensive understanding of blockchain and cryptocurrency, and how they can affect and benefit you and the world. You will also have the confidence and competence to use, invest, and benefit from blockchain and cryptocurrency, in a safe, smart, and responsible way.

SECTION 2

The History and Evolution of Blockchain and Cryptocurrency

Blockchain and cryptocurrency are not new or sudden inventions, but rather the results of a long and gradual process of innovation and experimentation that spans across decades, disciplines, and domains. They have been influenced and inspired by various ideas, events, and movements that have shaped and challenged the status quo of technology, finance, and society. They have also gone through different phases and stages that have marked their growth and development, as well as their successes and failures, as emerging and evolving technologies.

In this chapter, we will trace the history and evolution of blockchain and cryptocurrency, from the origins of blockchain and Bitcoin, to the rise and fall of the first wave of cryptocurrencies, to the emergence and growth of the second wave of cryptocurrencies, to the challenges and opportunities of the third wave of cryptocurrencies.

The Origins of Blockchain and Bitcoin

The origins of blockchain and Bitcoin can be traced back to the late 20th and early 21st centuries, when several concepts and technologies emerged and converged that laid the foundations and paved the way for the creation of blockchain and Bitcoin. Some of these concepts and technologies are:

- **Cryptography:** Cryptography is the science and art of creating and breaking codes that can protect and secure information and communication, from unauthorized access and manipulation. Cryptography has been used for centuries, for various purposes, such as military, diplomatic, political, and personal. However, cryptography became more relevant and important, with the advent of the digital age, when information and communication became more abundant and accessible, but also more vulnerable and exposed, to cyberattacks, hacks, and frauds. Cryptography provided the tools and techniques, such as encryption, hashing, and digital signatures, that enabled the creation and verification of secure and anonymous data and transactions, on the internet and beyond.

- **Cypherpunks:** Cypherpunks were a group of activists, hackers, and programmers, who advocated and promoted the use of cryptography, as a means of achieving social and political change, in the face of the increasing surveillance, censorship, and control, by the governments, corporations, and institutions, over the internet and society. Cypherpunks believed that cryptography could empower and protect the individuals and the communities, from the oppression and the interference, of the centralized and the powerful, by enabling them to create and exchange information and value, in a decentralized and distributed way. Cypherpunks created and experimented with various projects and platforms, such as anonymous remailers, digital cash, and electronic markets, that foreshadowed and influenced the development of blockchain and cryptocurrency.

- **Peer-to-peer networks:** Peer-to-peer networks were a type of networks, that allowed the direct and equal exchange of data and resources, among the nodes, or the peers, of the network, without the need for a central server, or a mediator, to coordinate and facilitate the exchange. Peer-to-peer networks were more efficient, resilient, and scalable, than the traditional client-server networks, as they could handle more traffic, avoid single points of failure, and adapt to changing conditions, by using the collective power and capacity of the nodes of the network. Peer-to-peer networks enabled the creation and distribution of various types of data and content, such as music, movies, and games, that challenged and disrupted the existing models and industries of technology and entertainment. Peer-to-peer networks also enabled the creation and transfer of various types of value and assets, such as currency, contracts, and identity, that challenged and disrupted the existing models and industries of finance and governance.

- **Bitcoin whitepaper:** Bitcoin whitepaper was a document, that was published in 2008, by an anonymous person or group, known as

Satoshi Nakamoto, that proposed and described a new and innovative system, of creating and exchanging digital currency, using blockchain technology. The whitepaper, titled "Bitcoin: A Peer-to-Peer Electronic Cash System", outlined the main principles and mechanisms, of how Bitcoin works, such as the creation of bitcoins, through a process called mining, the verification of transactions, through a process called proof-of-work, and the maintenance of a public and distributed ledger, called the blockchain. The whitepaper also addressed some of the main challenges and limitations, of the previous attempts and systems, of creating and exchanging digital currency, such as the double-spending problem, the scalability problem, and the trust problem. The whitepaper was the first and the most influential, of the many publications and contributions, that Satoshi Nakamoto made, to the development and the advancement of blockchain and cryptocurrency.

The Rise and Fall of the First Wave of Cryptocurrencies

The rise and fall of the first wave of cryptocurrencies can be marked by the period between 2009 and 2013, when Bitcoin was launched and adopted, as the first and the most successful cryptocurrency, that sparked the interest and the excitement, of the public and the media, as well as the innovation and the experimentation, of the developers and the entrepreneurs, in the field of blockchain and cryptocurrency. Some of the main events and milestones, of the first wave of cryptocurrencies, are:

- **Bitcoin launch:** Bitcoin launch was the event, that marked the beginning of the first wave of cryptocurrencies, when Bitcoin was officially released and activated, on January 3, 2009, by Satoshi Nakamoto, who mined the first block, or the genesis block, of the Bitcoin blockchain, that contained the message: "The Times 03/Jan/2009 Chancellor on brink of second bailout for banks". This message was a reference to the headline of The Times newspaper, which reported on the global financial crisis that was caused by the failure and the bailout of the banks and the financial institutions that Bitcoin aimed to replace and improve.

- **Bitcoin pizza:** Bitcoin pizza was the event, that marked the first real-world transaction, that used Bitcoin as a medium of exchange, when a user, named Laszlo Hanyecz, bought two pizzas, for 10,000 bitcoins, from another user, named Jeremy Sturdivant, on May 22, 2010. This event was a milestone that demonstrated the potential and the value of Bitcoin, as a digital currency that can be used to buy, sell, or trade, goods and services, online or offline. This event also became a legend that inspired and amused the Bitcoin community, as the value of the 10,000 bitcoins that were used to buy the pizzas, increased exponentially, over time, reaching billions of dollars, at some point.

- **Bitcoin bubble:** Bitcoin bubble was the event that marked the peak and the burst of the first wave of cryptocurrencies, when Bitcoin experienced a rapid and dramatic increase and decrease, in its price and popularity, in 2013. The price of Bitcoin rose from around \$13, at the beginning of the year, to around \$1,000, at the end of the year, reaching an all-time high, at that time, of \$1,242, on November 29, 2013. The popularity of Bitcoin also rose, as more and more users, investors, and media became aware and interested in Bitcoin, as a new and innovative technology, and as a lucrative and speculative investment. However, the price and the popularity of Bitcoin also fell, as several factors and events, such as technical issues, security breaches, regulatory actions, and market manipulations, affected and undermined the confidence and the stability of Bitcoin, as a reliable and secure technology, and as a viable and sustainable currency.

The Emergence and Growth of the Second Wave of Cryptocurrencies

The emergence and growth of the second wave of cryptocurrencies can be marked by the period between 2014 and 2017, when Ethereum was launched and adopted, as the second and the most influential cryptocurrency, that expanded and diversified, the scope and the scale, of the blockchain and cryptocurrency technology and ecosystem, beyond Bitcoin, and beyond currency. Some of the main events and milestones, of the second wave of cryptocurrencies, are:

- **Ethereum launch:** Ethereum launch was the event, that marked the beginning of the second wave of cryptocurrencies, when Ethereum was officially released and activated, on July 30, 2015, by Vitalik

Buterin, and a team of developers and researchers, who were part of the Ethereum Foundation, a non-profit organization, that was created to support and promote, the development and the advancement, of Ethereum. Ethereum was a new and innovative platform, that used blockchain technology, not only to create and exchange digital currency, called ether, but also to create and execute smart contracts, and decentralized applications, or , that could run on the Ethereum blockchain, and that could offer various types of services and solutions, for various sectors and domains, such as finance, business, governance, and society.

- **DAO hack:** DAO hack was the event, that marked the first major crisis and controversy, of the second wave of cryptocurrencies, when a hacker, or a group of hackers, exploited a vulnerability, in the code of a smart contract, called the DAO, or the Decentralized Autonomous Organization, that was created and launched, on the Ethereum platform, in 2016. The DAO was a complex and ambitious project, that aimed to create and operate, a decentralized and democratic organization, that could fund and manage, various projects and ventures, in the blockchain and cryptocurrency ecosystem, using the funds and the votes, of the DAO token holders, who were the members and the stakeholders, of the DAO. The hacker, or the hackers, managed to drain around $50 million worth of ether, from the DAO, by using a recursive function, that allowed them to repeatedly withdraw ether, from the DAO, before the balance was updated. This event was a shock and a scandal, that exposed and challenged, the security and the integrity, of the Ethereum platform, and the smart contracts, that ran on it, as well as the legality and the morality, of the blockchain and cryptocurrency technology and community, as a whole. The event also led to a split and a conflict, among the Ethereum community, over how to deal with and resolve the DAO hack, and the stolen funds. The split resulted in two versions, or forks, of the Ethereum blockchain, and the ether cryptocurrency, one that reversed and refunded, the DAO hack, and the stolen funds, called Ethereum, or ETH, and one that preserved and accepted, the DAO hack, and the stolen funds, called Ethereum Classic, or ETC.

- **ICO boom:** ICO boom was the event, that marked the peak and the burst, of the second wave of cryptocurrencies, when a new and innovative way, of creating and raising funds, for blockchain and cryptocurrency projects and ventures, emerged and exploded, in 2017. The ICO, or the Initial Coin Offering, was a process, that allowed the creators and the developers, of a new blockchain and cryptocurrency project and venture, to issue and sell, a new type of digital asset, called a token, to the public, in exchange for existing cryptocurrencies, such as ether, or bitcoin. The token was a representation, of the value, the utility, or the right, that the project and venture, offered and provided, to the token holders, who were the investors and the supporters, of the project and venture. The ICO was a fast and easy way of creating and raising funds, for blockchain and cryptocurrency projects and ventures, as it bypassed and avoided the traditional and regulated methods and institutions of creating and raising funds, such as banks, venture capitalists, or stock markets. The ICO also created and generated, a huge amount of interest and excitement, among the public and the media, as well as the innovation and the experimentation, among the developers and the entrepreneurs, in the field of blockchain and cryptocurrency. However, the ICO also created and generated a huge amount of risk and fraud, among the public and the media, as well as the regulation and the intervention, among the governments and the authorities, in the field of blockchain and cryptocurrency. Many of the ICOs, that were launched and conducted, in 2017, were either scams, or failures, that did not deliver, or fulfill, the promises and the expectations, that they made and raised, to the token holders, who lost their money, and their trust, in the ICOs, and the blockchain and cryptocurrency technology and ecosystem, as a whole.

The Challenges and Opportunities of the Third Wave of Cryptocurrencies

The challenges and opportunities of the third wave of cryptocurrencies can be marked by the period between 2018 and 2021, when Bitcoin and Ethereum, as well as other cryptocurrencies, faced and overcame, various difficulties and obstacles, that tested and threatened, their survival and growth, as well as introduced and implemented, various improvements and innovations, that enhanced and expanded, their functionality and performance, as well as their adoption and integration, in the mainstream and the society. Some of the main events and milestones, of the third wave of cryptocurrencies, are:

- **Bitcoin halving:** Bitcoin halving was the event, that marked the periodic and programmed, reduction and adjustment, of the reward, that the miners, or the nodes, of the Bitcoin network, received, for creating and adding, a new block, to the Bitcoin blockchain, and for verifying and confirming, the transactions, on the Bitcoin blockchain. The halving occurred every four years, or every 210,000 blocks, and it reduced the reward, by half, from 50 bitcoins, in 2009, to 25 bitcoins, in 2012, to 12.5 bitcoins, in 2016, to 6.25 bitcoins, in 2020. The halving was a mechanism that ensured and enforced, the scarcity and the deflation, of the bitcoin supply, that was limited and fixed, to 21 million bitcoins, that could ever be created and mined, by the Bitcoin network. The halving also affected and influenced, the price and the popularity, of Bitcoin, as a digital currency, and as a digital asset, as it created and increased, the demand and the value, of Bitcoin, among the users and the investors, who anticipated and speculated, on the effects and the outcomes, of the halving, on the Bitcoin market and ecosystem.

- **Ethereum 2.0:** Ethereum 2.0 was the event, that marked the major and ongoing, upgrade and transition, of the Ethereum platform, and the ether cryptocurrency, from the current and original version, called Ethereum 1.0, to a new and improved version, called Ethereum 2.0, that started and launched, in 2020, and that will continue and complete, in the next few years. Ethereum 2.0 was a complex and ambitious project, that aimed to address and solve, some of the main challenges and limitations, of Ethereum 1.0, such as the scalability, the security, and the sustainability, of the Ethereum platform, and the ether cryptocurrency, by introducing and implementing, various changes and enhancements, to the design, the architecture, the functionality, and the performance, of the Ethereum platform, and the ether cryptocurrency. Some of the main changes and enhancements, of Ethereum 2.0, are:

- o The transition from a proof-of-work, to a proof-of-stake, consensus mechanism, that will reduce and replace, the role and the power, of the miners, or the nodes, who create and add, the blocks, to the Ethereum blockchain, and who verify and confirm, the transactions, on the Ethereum blockchain, with the role and the power, of the validators, or the nodes, who stake, or lock, their own ether, to create and add, the blocks, to the Ethereum blockchain, and who verify and confirm, the transactions, on the Ethereum blockchain, based on their stake and reputation. This change will improve and increase, the efficiency, the security, and the decentralization, of the Ethereum platform, and the ether cryptocurrency, as well as the rewards and the incentives, for the validators, or the nodes, who participate and contribute, to the Ethereum network.

o The transition from a single and monolithic, to a multiple and modular, blockchain structure, that will split and divide, the Ethereum blockchain, into several smaller and parallel, blockchains, called shards, that will communicate and coordinate, with each other, and with a main and central, blockchain, called the beacon chain, that will manage and oversee, the shards, and the validators, or the nodes, of the Ethereum network. This change will improve and increase, the scalability, the capacity, and the performance, of the Ethereum platform, and the ether cryptocurrency, as well as the diversity and the flexibility, of the services and the solutions, that can be created and executed, on the Ethereum platform, and the ether cryptocurrency.

o The transition from a wasteful and harmful, to a sustainable and green, energy consumption and emission, that will reduce and minimize, the amount and the impact, of the energy and the resources, that are used and consumed, by the Ethereum platform, and the ether cryptocurrency, to run and operate, the Ethereum network, and the Ethereum blockchain. This change will improve and increase the sustainability, the responsibility, and the reputation of the Ethereum platform, and the ether cryptocurrency, as well as the awareness and the action of the users and the investors, who care and support the environment and the society.

- **DeFi boom:** DeFi boom was the event, that marked the emergence and the explosion, of a new and innovative sector and domain, of the blockchain and cryptocurrency technology and ecosystem, that expanded and diversified, the scope and the scale, of the blockchain and cryptocurrency technology and ecosystem, beyond currency, and beyond Ethereum, in 2020 and 2021. The DeFi, or the Decentralized Finance, was a sector and a domain, that aimed to create and offer, various types of financial services and products, such as lending, borrowing, saving, investing, trading, and more, using blockchain and cryptocurrency technology, and smart contracts, and decentralized applications, or dapps, that ran on various blockchain and cryptocurrency platforms, such as Ethereum, Binance Smart Chain, Solana, and more. The DeFi was a fast and growing sector and domain that attracted and generated a huge amount of interest and excitement, among the users and the investors, as well as the innovation and the experimentation, among the developers and the entrepreneurs, in the field of blockchain and cryptocurrency. The DeFi also created and generated a huge amount of value and wealth, among the users and the investors, as well as the regulation and the intervention, among the governments and the authorities, in the field of blockchain and cryptocurrency. Many of the DeFi projects and platforms, that were launched and conducted, in 2020 and 2021, were either successful, or failures, that delivered or fulfilled, the promises and the expectations, that they made and raised, to the users and the investors, who gained or lost, their money and their trust, in the DeFi, and the blockchain and cryptocurrency technology and ecosystem, as a whole.

In this chapter, you learned about the origins and development of blockchain and cryptocurrency, from the invention of Bitcoin by Satoshi Nakamoto to the emergence and growth of various altcoins and platforms. You also learned about the challenges and opportunities that each wave of innovation brought to the blockchain and cryptocurrency ecosystem. In the next chapter, we will discuss The Basics of Blockchain Technology.

SECTION 3

The Basics of Blockchain Technology

Blockchain technology is the core and the foundation of cryptocurrency technology, as well as many other applications and solutions, that use blockchain technology, to create and exchange value, data, and information, in a decentralized, distributed, and secure way. Blockchain technology is a system of records, or a ledger, that is shared and maintained, by a network of computers, or nodes, without the need for a central authority, intermediary, or trust. Blockchain technology has many features and benefits, such as immutability, transparency, verifiability, and more, that make it a powerful and revolutionary technology, for various sectors and domains, such as finance, business, governance, and society.

In this chapter, we will explain the basics of blockchain technology, such as how it works, what are its key features and benefits, what are its main types and components, and what are its common challenges and limitations.

How Blockchain Works?

Blockchain works by using a combination of cryptography, consensus, and network, to create and update a system of records, or a ledger, that contains information about transactions, events, or actions, that occur on the blockchain. A transaction, event, or action, is a transfer or an exchange, of value, data, or information, between two or more parties, or participants, on the blockchain. A transaction, event, or action, can be anything, such as sending or receiving currency, assets, contracts, identity, votes, and more, depending on the type and the purpose of the blockchain.

A transaction, event, or action, is recorded and stored, in a data structure, called a block, that contains the following information:

- The details of the transaction, event, or action, such as the sender, the receiver, the amount, the date, and the time.

- A cryptographic hash, or a unique code, that identifies and links the block to the previous block, in the blockchain, forming a chain of blocks, or a blockchain.

- A cryptographic signature, or a proof, that validates and confirms, the authenticity and the integrity, of the transaction, event, or action, and the block, using encryption, hashing, and digital signatures.

A block is created and added to the blockchain, by a computer, or a node, that is part of the network that supports and maintains the blockchain. A node can be any device, such as a computer, a smartphone, or a server, that is connected to the internet, and that runs a software, or a program, that allows it to communicate and interact, with the blockchain, and the other nodes, on the network. A node can have different roles and functions, on the network, such as creating and sending transactions, events, or actions, verifying and confirming transactions, events, or actions, creating and adding blocks, to the blockchain, storing and updating the blockchain, and more, depending on the type and the design, of the blockchain.

A block is created and added, to the blockchain, by using a consensus mechanism, or a set of rules, that ensures and enforces, that all the nodes, on the network, agree and accept, on the validity and the order, of the transactions, events, or actions, and the blocks, on the blockchain. A consensus mechanism can vary, depending on the type and the design, of the blockchain, but some of the most common and popular, consensus mechanisms, are:

- **Proof-of-work:** Proof-of-work is a consensus mechanism that requires the nodes to compete and solve a complex mathematical puzzle, using a lot of computational power and energy, to create and add a new block to the blockchain. The node, that solves the puzzle first, and creates and adds, the new block, to the blockchain, receives a reward, in the form of cryptocurrency, or digital assets, that are native, to the blockchain. Proof-of-work is used by blockchains, such as Bitcoin, and Ethereum 1.0, to ensure and enforce the security and the decentralization of the blockchain, and the cryptocurrency, or the digital assets, that run on it.

  o **Proof-of-stake:** Proof-of-stake is a consensus mechanism, that requires the nodes, to stake, or lock, a certain amount, of their own cryptocurrency, or digital assets, that are native, to the blockchain, to create and add, a new block, to the blockchain, based on their stake and reputation. The node that creates and adds the new block to the blockchain receives a reward, in the form of cryptocurrency, or digital assets, that are native, to the blockchain. Proof-of-stake is used by blockchains, such as Ethereum 2.0, and Cardano, to ensure and enforce the efficiency and the sustainability of the blockchain, and the cryptocurrency, or the digital assets, that run on it.

What are the Key Features and Benefits of Blockchain?

Blockchain has many features and benefits that make it a powerful and revolutionary technology, for various sectors and domains, such as finance, business, governance, and society. Some of the key features and benefits of blockchain are:

- **Immutability:** Immutability is the feature, that makes the blockchain, unchangeable and irreversible, meaning that once a transaction, event, or action, is recorded and stored, in a block, and the block, is added to the blockchain, it cannot be altered or deleted, by anyone, or anything, on the network, or outside the network. Immutability is the benefit, that makes the blockchain, reliable and trustworthy, meaning that the transactions, events, or actions, and the blocks, on the blockchain, are accurate and authentic, and that they can be verified and audited, by anyone, at any time, on the network, or outside the network.

- **Transparency:** Transparency is the feature, that makes the blockchain, visible and accessible, meaning that the transactions, events, or actions, and the blocks, on the blockchain, are public and open, and that they can be viewed and accessed, by anyone, at any time, on the network, or outside the network. Transparency is the benefit, that makes the blockchain, accountable and cooperative, meaning that the transactions, events, or actions, and the blocks, on the blockchain, are clear and honest, and that they can be monitored and evaluated, by anyone, at any time, on the network, or outside the network.

- **Verifiability:** Verifiability is the feature, that makes the blockchain, valid and confirmed, meaning that the transactions, events, or actions, and the blocks, on the blockchain, are checked and approved, by the nodes, on the network, using a consensus mechanism, or a set of rules, that ensures and enforces, that all the nodes, on the network, agree and accept, on the validity and the order, of the transactions, events, or actions, and the blocks, on the blockchain. Verifiability is the benefit, that makes the blockchain, secure and consistent, meaning that the transactions, events, or actions, and the blocks, on the blockchain, are protected and guaranteed, by the nodes, on the network, using cryptography, or a set of tools and techniques, that ensures and enforces, the authenticity and the integrity, of the transactions, events, or actions, and the blocks, on the blockchain.

What are the Main Types and Components of Blockchain?

Blockchain is not a single or uniform technology, but rather a family of technologies that can vary in terms of design, architecture, functionality, and performance. Some of the main types and components of blockchain are:

- **Public vs private blockchains:** A public blockchain is a type of blockchain, that is open and accessible, to anyone, who can join the network, view the blockchain, and participate in the transactions, events, or actions, on the blockchain, without the need for permission or identification. A public blockchain is more decentralized and distributed, but also less efficient and scalable, than a private blockchain. A private blockchain is a type of blockchain, that is closed and restricted, to a specific group of participants, who have the permission and the identification, to join the network, access the blockchain, and perform the transactions, events, or actions, on the blockchain. A private blockchain is more efficient and scalable, but also less decentralized and distributed, than a public blockchain.

- **Permissionless vs permissioned blockchains:** A permissionless blockchain is a type of public blockchain, where anyone can join the network, without the need for authorization or identification. A permissionless blockchain is more democratic and inclusive, but also more vulnerable and unstable, than a permissioned blockchain. A permissioned blockchain is a type of private blockchain, where participants need to be authorized and identified, by a central entity, or a consortium of entities, to join the network and perform the transactions, events, or actions, on the blockchain. A permissioned blockchain is more secure and reliable, but also more centralized and exclusive, than a permissionless blockchain.

- **Proof-of-work vs proof-of-stake blockchains:** Proof-of-work and proof-of-stake are two of the most common consensus mechanisms, or rules, that are used to validate and update the blocks on the blockchain. Proof-of-work requires the nodes to compete and solve a complex mathematical puzzle, using a lot of computational power and energy, to create and add a new block to the blockchain. Proof-of-work is more secure and decentralized, but also more wasteful and harmful, than proof-of-stake. Proof-of-stake requires the nodes to stake, or lock, a certain amount of their own cryptocurrency, or digital assets, that are native to the blockchain, to create and add a new block to the blockchain, based on their stake and reputation. Proof-of-stake is more efficient and sustainable, but also more elitist and oligarchic, than proof-of-work.

What are the Common Challenges and Limitations of Blockchain?

Blockchain is not a perfect or flawless technology, but rather a developing and evolving technology that faces and encounters various challenges and limitations that affect and limit its functionality and performance, as well as its adoption and integration, in the mainstream and the society. Some of the common challenges and limitations of blockchain are:

- **Scalability:** Scalability is the challenge and the limitation, that affects and limits, the ability and the capacity, of the blockchain, to handle and process, a large and increasing, number and volume, of transactions, events, or actions, on the blockchain, in a fast and smooth, way. Scalability is affected and limited, by various factors and parameters, such as the size and the frequency, of the blocks, on the blockchain, the speed and the bandwidth, of the network, that supports and maintains, the blockchain, and the complexity and the diversity, of the transactions, events, or actions, on the blockchain. Scalability is a trade-off and a balance, between the security and the efficiency, of the blockchain, as increasing the scalability, may compromise the security, and vice versa.

- **Interoperability:** Interoperability is the challenge and the limitation, that affects and limits, the ability and the capacity, of the blockchain, to communicate and interact, with other blockchains, and with other systems and platforms, that are not based on blockchain technology, in a seamless and compatible, way. Interoperability is affected and limited, by the variety and the diversity, of the design, the architecture, the functionality, and the performance, of the different blockchains, and the different systems and platforms, that exist and operate, in the blockchain and cryptocurrency technology and ecosystem, and in the mainstream and the society. Interoperability is a requirement and a goal, for the blockchain, to achieve and realize, its full potential and value, as a universal and versatile, technology, that can offer and provide, various types of services and solutions, for various sectors and domains, such as finance, business, governance, and society.

- **Regulation:** Regulation is the challenge and the limitation, that affects and limits, the ability and the capacity, of the blockchain, to comply and conform, with the laws, norms, and values, of the existing and the emerging, systems and institutions, that govern and regulate, the technology, the finance, and the society, in the mainstream and the society. Regulation is affected and limited, by the uncertainty and the ambiguity, of the status and the nature, of the blockchain, and the cryptocurrency, or the digital assets, that run on it, as well as the complexity and the diversity, of the transactions, events, or actions, that occur on it, in terms of their legality, their ethics, and their impact, on the technology, the finance, and the society. Regulation is a challenge and a balance, for the blockchain, to achieve and maintain, its innovation and its disruption, as well as its integration and its acceptance, in the mainstream and the society.

In this chapter, you learned about the core principles and mechanisms of blockchain technology, and how it enables a decentralized, distributed, and secure network of transactions and records. You also learned about the key features and benefits of blockchain, such as transparency, immutability, and consensus. You also learned about the main types and components of blockchain, such as public and private blockchains, nodes, miners, and smart contracts. You also learned about the common challenges and limitations of blockchain, such as scalability, interoperability, and energy consumption.

SECTION 4

The Basics of Cryptocurrency Technology

Cryptocurrency technology is the core and the application of blockchain technology, as well as many other technologies, that are used to create and exchange digital currency, that can be used to buy, sell, or trade goods and services, online or offline, without the need for a central authority, intermediary, or trust. Cryptocurrency technology is a medium of exchange, a store of value, and a unit of account, that has many features and benefits, such as decentralization, security, anonymity, speed, and more, that make it a powerful and revolutionary technology, for various sectors and domains, such as finance, business, governance, and society.

In this chapter, we will explain the basics of cryptocurrency technology, such as how it works, what are its key features and benefits, what are its main types and components, and what are its common challenges and limitations.

How Cryptocurrency Works?

Cryptocurrency works by using a combination of cryptography, consensus, and network, to create and transfer digital currency that is based on blockchain technology. A digital currency, or a coin, is a unit of value, that can be used to buy, sell, or trade goods and services, online or offline, without the need for a central authority, intermediary, or trust. A digital currency, or a coin, can be anything, such as Bitcoin, Ethereum, Litecoin, and more, depending on the type and the purpose of the cryptocurrency.

A digital currency, or a coin, is created and transferred, by using a data structure, called a transaction, that contains the following information:

- The details of the transaction, such as the sender, the receiver, the amount, the date, and the time.

- A cryptographic hash, or a unique code, that identifies and links the transaction to the previous transaction, in the blockchain, forming a chain of transactions, or a blockchain.

- A cryptographic signature, or a proof, that validates and confirms, the authenticity and the integrity, of the transaction, and the coin, using encryption, hashing, and digital signatures.

A transaction is created and transferred, by a user, or a participant, who is part of the network that supports and maintains the cryptocurrency. A user can be any person, or entity, that is connected to the internet, and that has a software, or a program, called a wallet, that allows them to create and send transactions, and to store and receive coins, on the network. A user can have different roles and functions, on the network, such as creating and sending transactions, verifying and confirming transactions, creating and adding blocks to the blockchain, storing and updating the blockchain, and more, depending on the type and the design of the cryptocurrency.

A transaction is created and transferred, by using a consensus mechanism, or a set of rules, that ensures and enforces that all the users, on the network, agree and accept, on the validity and the order, of the transactions, and the coins, on the blockchain. A consensus mechanism can vary, depending on the type and the design, of the cryptocurrency, but some of the most common and popular, consensus mechanisms, are:

- **Proof-of-work:** Proof-of-work is a consensus mechanism that requires the users to compete and solve a complex mathematical puzzle, using a lot of computational power and energy, to create and transfer a new coin, or a block of transactions, to the blockchain. The user that solves the puzzle first, and creates and transfers, the new coin, or the block of transactions, to the blockchain, receives a reward, in the form of cryptocurrency, or digital assets, that are native, to the cryptocurrency. Proof-of-work is used by cryptocurrencies, such as Bitcoin, and Ethereum 1.0, to ensure and enforce the security and the decentralization of the cryptocurrency, and the digital assets that run on it.

- **Proof-of-stake:** Proof-of-stake is a consensus mechanism, that requires the users, to stake, or lock, a certain amount, of their own cryptocurrency, or digital assets, that are native, to the cryptocurrency, to create and transfer, a new coin, or a block of transactions, to the blockchain, based on their stake and reputation. The user that creates and transfers the new coin, or the block of transactions, to the blockchain, receives a reward, in the form of cryptocurrency, or digital assets, that are native, to the cryptocurrency. Proof-of-stake is used by cryptocurrencies, such as Ethereum 2.0, and Cardano, to ensure and enforce the efficiency and the sustainability of the cryptocurrency, and the digital assets that run on it.

What are the Key Features and Benefits of Cryptocurrency?

Cryptocurrency has many features and benefits that make it a powerful and revolutionary technology, for various sectors and domains, such as finance, business, governance, and society. Some of the key features and benefits of cryptocurrency are:

- **Decentralization:** Decentralization is the feature, that makes the cryptocurrency, independent and autonomous, meaning that it is not controlled or issued, by any single entity, such as a government, a bank, or a corporation, but rather by the network of users, who collectively manage and maintain, the cryptocurrency system. Decentralization is the benefit, that makes the cryptocurrency, inclusive and democratic, meaning that it gives the power and the freedom, to the users, to create and exchange value, data, and information, in a peer-to-peer way, without the need for intermediaries, such as banks, brokers, or agents, reducing costs, delays, and risks.

- **Security:** Security is the feature, that makes the cryptocurrency, protected and encrypted, meaning that it uses cryptography, or a set of tools and techniques, to secure and safeguard, the transactions and the coins, from fraud, theft, or hacking, by using encryption, hashing, and digital signatures. Security is the benefit, that makes the cryptocurrency, reliable and trustworthy, meaning that it ensures and guarantees, the authenticity and the integrity, of the transactions and the coins, and that it can be verified and audited, by anyone, at any time, on the network, or outside the network.

- **Anonymity:** Anonymity is the feature, that makes the cryptocurrency, private and pseudonymous, meaning that it does not reveal or expose, the personal and sensitive information and activities, of the users, such as their names, addresses, or identities, but rather uses random and unique codes, or addresses, to identify and link, the transactions and the coins, on the blockchain. Anonymity is the benefit, that makes the cryptocurrency, confidential and discreet, meaning that it protects and respects, the privacy and the preferences, of the users, who can choose and control, how much and what kind of information and activities, they want to share and disclose, on the network, or outside the network.

- **Speed:** Speed is the feature, that makes the cryptocurrency, fast and instant, meaning that it can process and confirm transactions, in a matter of minutes, or even seconds, with minimal or no fees, compared to traditional payment systems, that can take days, or even weeks, and charge high fees, to process and confirm transactions. Speed is the benefit, that makes the cryptocurrency, convenient and accessible, meaning that it enables and facilitates, the creation and exchange of value, data, and information, across the globe, at any time, and at any place, without the need for intermediaries, such as banks, brokers, or agents, reducing costs, delays, and risks.

What are the Main Types and Components of Cryptocurrency?

Cryptocurrency is not a single or uniform currency, but rather a family of currencies that can vary in terms of design, functionality, and performance. Some of the main types and components of cryptocurrency are:

- **Bitcoin vs altcoins:** Bitcoin is the first and the most popular cryptocurrency, that was created in 2009, by an anonymous person or group, known as Satoshi Nakamoto. It is based on a public, permissionless, and proof-of-work blockchain that has a maximum supply of 21 million bitcoins. Bitcoin is the most widely used and accepted cryptocurrency, that can be used as a medium of exchange, a store of value, and a unit of account, for various goods and services, online or offline. Altcoins are alternative cryptocurrencies that were created after Bitcoin, either by modifying or improving some aspects of Bitcoin, or by creating a completely new and different cryptocurrency. There are thousands of altcoins, such as Ethereum, Litecoin, Ripple, and more, each with its own features and advantages, that can be used for various purposes and functions, such as smart contracts, decentralized applications, or digital assets.

- **Tokens vs coins:** Tokens and coins are two types of digital assets that can be created and exchanged using blockchain and cryptocurrency technology. Coins are native to their own blockchain, and can be used as a currency, or a fuel, to power the blockchain. Tokens are created on top of an existing blockchain, and can represent a variety of things, such as assets, rights, services, or utilities. Tokens can be classified into different categories, such as utility tokens, security tokens, governance tokens, and more, depending on their purpose and function.

- **Stablecoins vs volatile coins:** Stablecoins and volatile coins are two types of cryptocurrencies that differ in terms of their price stability and volatility. Stablecoins are cryptocurrencies that are pegged, or linked, to a stable asset, such as a fiat currency, a commodity, or a basket of assets, to maintain a stable and predictable value. Volatile coins are cryptocurrencies that are not pegged, or linked, to any stable asset, and that can experience significant and unpredictable fluctuations in their value, depending on the market forces of supply and demand.

What are the Common Challenges and Limitations of Cryptocurrency?

Cryptocurrency is not a perfect or flawless currency, but rather a developing and evolving currency that faces and encounters various challenges and limitations that affect and limit its functionality and performance, as well as its adoption and integration, in the mainstream and the society. Some of the common challenges and limitations of cryptocurrency are:

- **Security:** Security is the challenge and the limitation, that affects and limits, the ability and the capacity, of the cryptocurrency, to protect and safeguard, the transactions and the coins, from cyberattacks, hacks, thefts, and frauds, that can compromise the integrity, availability, and confidentiality, of the data and the assets, on the network, or outside the network. Security is affected and limited, by various factors and events, such as technical issues, human errors, malicious actors, and market manipulations, that can exploit and expose, the vulnerabilities and the weaknesses, of the cryptocurrency, and the blockchain, that run on it, as well as the users and the investors, who use and own it.

- **Privacy:** Privacy is the challenge and the limitation that affects and limits the ability and the capacity, of the cryptocurrency, to respect and protect, the personal and sensitive information and activities, of the users, on the network, or outside the network. Privacy is affected and limited, by various factors and events, such as regulatory actions, legal disputes, social norms, and ethical values, that can demand and require, the disclosure and the exposure, of the information and the activities, of the users, on the network, or outside the network, for various purposes and reasons, such as taxation, compliance, investigation, or identification.

- **Regulation:** Regulation is the challenge and the limitation, that affects and limits, the ability and the capacity, of the cryptocurrency, to comply and conform, with the laws, norms, and values, of the existing and the emerging, systems and institutions, that govern and regulate, the technology, the finance, and the society, in the mainstream and the society. Regulation is affected and limited, by the uncertainty and the ambiguity, of the status and the nature, of the cryptocurrency, and the blockchain, that run on it, as well as the complexity and the diversity, of the transactions and the coins, that occur on it, in terms of their legality, their ethics, and their impact, on the technology, the finance, and the society. Regulation is a challenge and a balance, for the cryptocurrency, to achieve and maintain, its innovation and its disruption, as well as its integration and its acceptance, in the mainstream and the society.

In this chapter, you learned about the core principles and mechanisms of cryptocurrency technology, and how it enables a digital, peer-to-peer, and trustless medium of exchange and store of value. You also learned about the key features and benefits of cryptocurrency, such as anonymity, fungibility, and divisibility. You also learned about the main types and components of cryptocurrency, such as coins and tokens, wallets and keys, and exchanges and markets. You also learned about the common challenges and limitations of cryptocurrency, such as volatility, security, and regulation.

SECTION 5

The Blockchain and Cryptocurrency Ecosystem

Blockchain and cryptocurrency are not isolated or independent technologies, but rather interconnected and interdependent technologies, that form and shape, a complex and dynamic ecosystem, that consists of various players and stakeholders, platforms and applications, trends and developments, and issues and debates, that interact and influence each other, and the technology, the finance, and the society, in the mainstream and the society.

In this chapter, we will describe and analyze the blockchain and cryptocurrency ecosystem, such as who are the key players and stakeholders, what are the main platforms and applications, what are the main trends and developments, and what are the main issues and debates, in the blockchain and cryptocurrency ecosystem, and how they affect and benefit, the technology, the finance, and the society.

Who are the Key Players and Stakeholders in the Blockchain and Cryptocurrency Ecosystem?

The blockchain and cryptocurrency ecosystem is composed of various players and stakeholders, who have different roles and functions, interests and motivations, perspectives and opinions, on the blockchain and cryptocurrency technology and ecosystem, and who contribute and participate, in various ways and levels, to the creation and exchange, of value, data, and information, on the blockchain and cryptocurrency technology and ecosystem. Some of the key players and stakeholders in the blockchain and cryptocurrency ecosystem are:

- **Users:** Users are the individuals or entities, who use and own, the blockchain and cryptocurrency technology and ecosystem, to create and exchange value, data, and information, for various purposes and functions, such as buying, selling, or trading goods and services, online or offline, investing, saving, or donating money, online or offline, creating and executing smart contracts, or decentralized applications, online or offline, and more. Users can be classified into different categories, such as consumers, investors, developers, and more, depending on their purpose and function, on the blockchain and cryptocurrency technology and ecosystem.

- **Nodes:** Nodes are the devices, such as computers, smartphones, or servers, that are connected to the internet, and that run a software, or a program, that allows them to communicate and interact, with the blockchain and cryptocurrency technology and ecosystem, and with the other nodes, on the network, that supports and maintains, the blockchain and cryptocurrency technology and ecosystem. Nodes can have different roles and functions, on the network, such as creating and sending transactions, events, or actions, verifying and confirming transactions, events, or actions, creating and adding blocks, to the blockchain, storing and updating the blockchain, and more, depending on the type and the design, of the blockchain and cryptocurrency technology and ecosystem.

- **Miners:** Miners are a type of nodes, that use a lot of computational power and energy, to compete and solve, a complex mathematical puzzle, using a consensus mechanism, called proof-of-work, to create and add, a new block, to the blockchain, and to verify and confirm, the transactions, events, or actions, on the blockchain. Miners receive a reward, in the form of cryptocurrency, or digital assets, that are native, to the blockchain, for creating and adding a new block to the blockchain. Miners ensure and enforce, the security and the decentralization, of the blockchain and cryptocurrency technology and ecosystem, as well as the creation and the distribution, of the cryptocurrency, or the digital assets, that run on it.

- **Validators:** Validators are a type of nodes, that stake, or lock, a certain amount, of their own cryptocurrency, or digital assets, that are native, to the blockchain, to create and add, a new block, to the blockchain, and to verify and confirm, the transactions, events, or actions, on the blockchain, based on their stake and reputation, using a consensus mechanism, called proof-of-stake. Validators receive a reward, in the form of cryptocurrency, or digital assets, that are native, to the blockchain, for creating and adding a new block to the blockchain. Validators ensure and enforce the efficiency and the sustainability of the blockchain and cryptocurrency technology and ecosystem, as well as the rewards and the incentives, for the nodes, who participate and contribute to the network.

- **Exchanges:** Exchanges are platforms or applications, that allow the users, to buy, sell, or trade, cryptocurrencies, or digital assets, for other cryptocurrencies, or digital assets, or for fiat currencies, or traditional assets, such as dollars, euros, or gold, using various methods and mechanisms, such as market orders, limit orders, or peer-to-peer transactions. Exchanges can be classified into different categories, such as centralized exchanges, decentralized exchanges, or hybrid exchanges, depending on their design and architecture, on the blockchain and cryptocurrency technology and ecosystem.

- **Wallets:** Wallets are software or hardware that allow the users to store and manage their cryptocurrencies, or digital assets, on the blockchain and cryptocurrency technology and ecosystem. Wallets can be classified into different categories, such as hot wallets, cold wallets, or paper wallets, depending on their security and accessibility, on the blockchain and cryptocurrency technology and ecosystem.

- **Developers:** Developers are individuals or entities, who create and develop various platforms and applications, that use and offer various services and solutions, based on the blockchain and cryptocurrency technology and ecosystem, for various sectors and domains, such as finance, business, governance, and society. Developers can be classified into different categories, such as core developers, who work on the design and the architecture, of the blockchain and cryptocurrency technology and ecosystem, application developers, who work on the functionality and the performance, of the platforms and applications, that use and offer, various services and solutions, based on the blockchain and cryptocurrency technology and ecosystem, and more, depending on their role and function, on the blockchain and cryptocurrency technology and ecosystem.

- **Entrepreneurs:** Entrepreneurs are individuals or entities, who create and launch various projects and ventures, that use and offer various services and solutions, based on the blockchain and cryptocurrency technology and ecosystem, for various sectors and domains, such as finance, business, governance, and society. Entrepreneurs can be classified into different categories, such as founders, who initiate and lead, the projects and ventures, that use and offer, various services and solutions, based on the blockchain and cryptocurrency technology and ecosystem, investors, who fund and support, the projects and ventures, that use and offer, various services and solutions, based on the blockchain and cryptocurrency technology and ecosystem, and more, depending on their role and function, on the blockchain and cryptocurrency technology and ecosystem.

- **Governments:** Governments are institutions or organizations that govern and regulate technology, the finance, and the society, in the mainstream and the society. Governments can have different roles and functions, on the blockchain and cryptocurrency technology and ecosystem, such as enforcers, who create and implement, the laws, norms, and values, that affect and limit, the blockchain and cryptocurrency technology and ecosystem, such as taxation, compliance, investigation, or identification, supporters, who promote and encourage, the blockchain and cryptocurrency technology and ecosystem, such as innovation, education, adoption, or integration, and more, depending on their perspective and opinion, on the blockchain and cryptocurrency technology and ecosystem.

What are the Main Platforms and Applications of Blockchain and Cryptocurrency?

The blockchain and cryptocurrency technology and ecosystem is composed of various platforms and applications that use and offer various services and solutions, based on the blockchain and cryptocurrency technology and ecosystem, for various sectors and domains, such as finance, business, governance, and society. Some of the main platforms and applications of blockchain and cryptocurrency are:

- **Bitcoin:** Bitcoin is the first and the most popular platform and application, of blockchain and cryptocurrency technology and ecosystem, that was created in 2009, by an anonymous person or group, known as Satoshi Nakamoto. It is based on a public, permissionless, and proof-of-work blockchain that has a maximum supply of 21 million bitcoins. Bitcoin is the most widely used and accepted cryptocurrency, that can be used as a medium of exchange, a store of value, and a unit of account, for various goods and services, online or offline.

- **Ethereum:** Ethereum is the second and the most influential platform and application, of blockchain and cryptocurrency technology and ecosystem, that was created in 2015, by Vitalik Buterin, and a team of developers and researchers, who were part of the Ethereum Foundation, a non-profit organization, that was created to support and promote, the development and the advancement, of Ethereum. It is based on a public, permissionless, and proof-of-work blockchain that is transitioning to a proof-of-stake blockchain, called Ethereum 2.0, that will be completed in the next few years. Ethereum is a platform, that uses blockchain technology, not only to create and exchange digital currency, called ether, but also to create and execute smart contracts, and decentralized applications, or dapps, that can run on the Ethereum blockchain, and that can offer various types of services and solutions, for various sectors and domains, such as finance, business, governance, and society.

- **DeFi:** DeFi, or Decentralized Finance, is a sector and a domain, of the blockchain and cryptocurrency technology and ecosystem, that emerged and exploded, in 2020 and 2021, that aims to create and offer, various types of financial services and products, such as lending, borrowing, saving, investing, trading, and more, using blockchain and cryptocurrency technology, and smart contracts, and decentralized applications, or dapps, that run on various blockchain and cryptocurrency platforms, such as Ethereum, Binance Smart Chain, Solana, and more. DeFi is a fast growing sector and domain that attracts and generates a huge amount of interest and excitement, among the users and the investors, as well as the innovation and the experimentation, among the developers and the entrepreneurs, in the field of blockchain and cryptocurrency. DeFi also creates and generates a huge amount of value and wealth, among the users and the investors, as well as the regulation and the intervention, among the governments and the authorities, in the field of blockchain and cryptocurrency. Some of the main platforms and applications, of DeFi, are:

- o **Uniswap:** Uniswap is a platform and an application, of DeFi, that allows the users, to exchange, or swap, any two tokens, or digital assets, that are based on the Ethereum blockchain, without the need for intermediaries, such as exchanges, brokers, or agents, using a mechanism, called an automated market maker, or AMM, that uses liquidity pools, or pools of tokens, or digital assets, that are provided by the users, who receive fees, in return, for providing liquidity, to the platform and the application.

- o **Compound:** Compound is a platform and an application, of DeFi, that allows the users, to lend and borrow, any tokens, or digital assets, that are based on the Ethereum blockchain, without the need for intermediaries, such as banks, lenders, or borrowers, using a mechanism, called a money market, or a market, that uses supply and demand, to determine the interest rates, for lending and borrowing, the tokens, or the digital assets, on the platform and the application.

○ **Aave:** Aave is a platform and an application, of DeFi, that allows the users, to lend and borrow, any tokens, or digital assets, that are based on the Ethereum blockchain, without the need for intermediaries, such as banks, lenders, or borrowers, using a mechanism, called a flash loan, or a loan, that allows the users, to borrow, any amount of tokens, or digital assets, without any collateral, or security, as long as they repay, the loan, within the same transaction, or block, on the platform and the application.

What are the Main Trends and Developments in the Blockchain and Cryptocurrency Ecosystem?

The blockchain and cryptocurrency ecosystem is a complex and dynamic ecosystem that is constantly evolving and changing, in response to various factors and events, that affect and influence, the technology, the finance, and the society, in the mainstream and the society. Some of the main trends and developments in the blockchain and cryptocurrency ecosystem are:

- **NFTs:** NFTs, or Non-Fungible Tokens, are a type of digital asset, that are based on blockchain and cryptocurrency technology, that represent and certify, the ownership and the uniqueness, of a digital or physical item, such as art, music, games, collectibles, and more, using a mechanism, called a tokenization, or a process, that converts and assigns, a digital or physical item, into a token, or a digital asset, that can be stored and transferred, on the blockchain and cryptocurrency technology and ecosystem. NFTs are a new and innovative trend and development, in the blockchain and cryptocurrency ecosystem, that emerged and exploded, in 2020 and 2021, that attracts and generates, a huge amount of interest and excitement, among the users and the investors, as well as the innovation and the experimentation, among the developers and the entrepreneurs, in the field of blockchain and cryptocurrency. NFTs also create and generate a huge amount of value and wealth, among the users and the investors, as well as the regulation and the intervention, among the governments and the authorities, in the field of blockchain and cryptocurrency. Some of the main platforms and applications, of NFTs, are:

- ○ OpenSea: OpenSea is a platform and an application, of NFTs, that allows the users, to buy, sell, or trade, any NFTs, or digital assets, that are based on the Ethereum blockchain, or other blockchains, that support NFTs, such as Polygon, Flow, or Tezos, using various methods and mechanisms, such as auctions, bundles, or collections, on the platform and the application.

- ○ CryptoPunks: CryptoPunks are a platform and an application, of NFTs, that are based on the Ethereum blockchain, that consist of 10,000 unique and pixelated characters, or punks, that are randomly generated, and that have different attributes and traits, such as skin color, hair style, accessories, and more, on the platform and the application. CryptoPunks are one of the first and the most popular NFTs, or digital assets, that are based on the Ethereum blockchain, that have a high and increasing value and demand, among the users and the investors, on the platform and the application.

o NBA Top Shot: NBA Top Shot is a platform and an application, of NFTs, that are based on the Flow blockchain, that consist of digital video clips, or moments, that capture and highlight, the best and the most memorable plays, or actions, of the NBA, or the

National Basketball Association, the professional basketball league, in the United States and Canada, on the platform and the application. NBA Top Shot is a new and innovative NFTs, or digital assets, that are based on the Flow blockchain, that have a high and increasing value and demand, among the users and the investors, especially the fans and the enthusiasts, of the NBA, and the basketball, on the platform and the application.

- **CBDCs:** CBDCs, or Central Bank Digital Currencies, are a type of digital currency, that are based on blockchain and cryptocurrency technology, that are issued and controlled, by a central bank, or a monetary authority, of a country, or a region, that can be used as a legal tender, or a official currency, for various purposes and functions, such as payments, settlements, remittances, and more, on the blockchain and cryptocurrency technology and ecosystem. CBDCs are a new and emerging trend and development, in the blockchain and cryptocurrency ecosystem, that emerged and evolved, in 2020 and 2021, that attracts and generates, a huge amount of interest and attention, among the governments and the authorities, as well as the innovation and the experimentation, among the developers and the researchers, in the field of blockchain and cryptocurrency. CBDCs also create and generate a huge amount of opportunities and challenges, among the governments and the authorities, as well as the users and the investors, in the field of blockchain and cryptocurrency. Some of the main platforms and applications, of CBDCs, are:

○ **DCEP:** DCEP, or Digital Currency Electronic Payment, is a platform and an application, of CBDCs, that are based on blockchain and cryptocurrency technology, that are issued and controlled, by the People's Bank of China, or the central bank, of China, that can be used as a legal tender, or a official currency, for various purposes and functions, such as payments, settlements, remittances, and more, on the blockchain and cryptocurrency technology and ecosystem. DCEP is one of the first and the most advanced CBDCs, or digital currencies, that are based on blockchain and cryptocurrency technology, that have been launched and tested, in various cities and regions, in China, such as Beijing, Shanghai, Shenzhen, and more, on the platform and the application.

- ○ **e-Krona:** e-Krona is a platform and an application, of CBDCs, that are based on blockchain and cryptocurrency technology, that are issued and controlled, by the Sveriges Riksbank, or the central bank, of Sweden, that can be used as a legal tender, or a official currency, for various purposes and functions, such as payments, settlements, remittances, and more, on the blockchain and cryptocurrency technology and ecosystem. e-Krona is one of the first and the most progressive CBDCs, or digital currencies, that are based on blockchain and cryptocurrency technology, that have been developed and piloted, in various scenarios and environments, in Sweden, such as retail, wholesale, online, offline, and more, on the platform and the application.

What are the Main Issues and Debates in the Blockchain and Cryptocurrency Ecosystem?

The blockchain and cryptocurrency ecosystem is a complex and dynamic ecosystem that is constantly facing and encountering various issues and debates, that affect and influence, the technology, the finance, and the society, in the mainstream and the society. Some of the main issues and debates in the blockchain and cryptocurrency ecosystem are:

- **Energy consumption and emission:** Energy consumption and emission is an issue and a debate, that affects and influences, the ability and the capacity, of the blockchain and cryptocurrency technology and ecosystem, to run and operate, the network and the blockchain, that supports and maintains, the blockchain and cryptocurrency technology and ecosystem, in a sustainable and green way. Energy consumption and emission is affected and influenced, by the amount and the impact, of the energy and the resources, that are used and consumed, by the blockchain and cryptocurrency technology and ecosystem, to run and operate, the network and the blockchain, especially by the nodes, who use a consensus mechanism, called proof-of-work, to create and add, new blocks, to the blockchain, and to verify and confirm, the transactions, events, or actions, on the blockchain. Energy consumption and emission is a trade-off and a balance, between the security and the efficiency, of the blockchain and cryptocurrency technology and ecosystem, as reducing the energy consumption and emission, may compromise the security, and vice versa.

- **Regulation and compliance:** Regulation and compliance is an issue and a debate, that affects and influences, the ability and the capacity, of the blockchain and cryptocurrency technology and ecosystem, to comply and conform, with the laws, norms, and values, of the existing and the emerging, systems and institutions, that govern and regulate, the technology, the finance, and the society, in the mainstream and the society. Regulation and compliance is affected and influenced, by the uncertainty and the ambiguity, of the status and the nature, of the blockchain and cryptocurrency technology and ecosystem, as well as the complexity and the diversity, of the transactions, events, or actions, and the coins, or the digital assets, that occur and exist, on the blockchain and cryptocurrency technology and ecosystem, in terms of their legality, their ethics, and their impact, on the technology, the finance, and the society. Regulation and compliance is a challenge and a balance, for the blockchain and cryptocurrency technology and ecosystem, to achieve and maintain, its innovation and its disruption, as well as its integration and its acceptance, in the mainstream and the society.

- **Adoption and integration:** Adoption and integration is an issue and a debate, that affects and influences, the ability and the capacity, of the blockchain and cryptocurrency technology and ecosystem, to be used and accepted, by the users and the investors, as well as the platforms and the applications, that use and offer, various services and solutions, based on the blockchain and cryptocurrency technology and ecosystem, for various sectors and domains, such as finance, business, governance, and society, in the mainstream and the society. Adoption and integration is affected and influenced, by the awareness and the education, of the users and the investors, as well as the platforms and the applications, that use and offer, various services and solutions, based on the blockchain and cryptocurrency technology and ecosystem, about the features and the benefits, as well as the challenges and the limitations, of the blockchain and cryptocurrency technology and ecosystem, as well as the compatibility and the interoperability, of the blockchain and cryptocurrency technology and ecosystem, with the existing and the emerging, systems and platforms, that are not based on blockchain and cryptocurrency technology, in the mainstream and the society. Adoption and integration is a requirement and a goal, for the blockchain and cryptocurrency technology and ecosystem, to achieve and realize, its full potential and value, as a universal and versatile, technology, that can offer and provide, various types of services and solutions, for various sectors and domains, such as finance, business, governance, and society.

In this chapter, you learned about the key players and stakeholders in the blockchain and cryptocurrency ecosystem, such as users, investors, developers, regulators, and media. You also learned about the main platforms and applications of blockchain and cryptocurrency, such as Ethereum, DeFi, NFTs, and CBDCs. You also learned about the main trends and developments in the blockchain and cryptocurrency ecosystem, such as adoption, innovation, and competition. You also learned about the main issues and debates in the blockchain and cryptocurrency ecosystem, such as governance, ethics, and social impact.

SECTION 6

The Future of Blockchain and Cryptocurrency

Blockchain and cryptocurrency are not static or stagnant technologies, but rather dynamic and adaptive technologies that are constantly evolving and changing, in response to various factors and events, that affect and influence, the technology, the finance, and the society, in the mainstream and the society. Blockchain and cryptocurrency have the potential and the possibility, to create and generate, various impacts and implications, for the society, the economy, and the environment, as well as to offer and provide, various use cases and opportunities, for various sectors and domains, such as finance, business, governance, and society. However, blockchain and cryptocurrency also face and encounter various risks and challenges, for the security, the privacy, and the regulation, of the technology, the finance, and the society, in the mainstream and the society. Therefore, blockchain and cryptocurrency require and demand, various best practices and recommendations, for the users, the investors, and the developers, who use and own, the blockchain and cryptocurrency technology and ecosystem, to ensure and enhance, the functionality and the performance, as well as the adoption and the integration, of the blockchain and cryptocurrency technology and ecosystem, in the mainstream and the society.

In this chapter, we will explore and discuss the future of blockchain and cryptocurrency, such as what are the potential impacts and implications, of blockchain and cryptocurrency, for the society, the economy, and the environment, what are the emerging and innovative use cases and opportunities, of blockchain and cryptocurrency, what are the risks and challenges, of blockchain and cryptocurrency, for the security, the privacy, and the regulation, and what are the best practices and recommendations, for blockchain and cryptocurrency users, investors, and developers.

What are the Potential Impacts and Implications of Blockchain and Cryptocurrency for Society, Economy, and Environment?

Blockchain and cryptocurrency have the potential and the possibility, to create and generate, various impacts and implications, for the society, the economy, and the environment, in the mainstream and the society. Some of the potential impacts and implications of blockchain and cryptocurrency are:

- **Society:** Blockchain and cryptocurrency have the potential and the possibility, to create and generate, various impacts and implications, for the society, in the mainstream and the society, such as:

  - **Inclusion and empowerment:** Blockchain and cryptocurrency have the potential and the possibility, to create and generate, inclusion and empowerment, for the society, in the mainstream and the society, by providing and enabling, access and participation, to the blockchain and cryptocurrency technology and ecosystem, for the people and the communities, who are excluded or marginalized, from the existing and the emerging, systems and platforms, that govern and regulate, the technology, the finance, and the society, such as the unbanked, the underprivileged, the oppressed, and more, who can use and benefit, from the blockchain and cryptocurrency technology and ecosystem, to create and exchange value, data, and information, in a peer-to-peer way, without the need for intermediaries, such as banks, brokers, or agents, reducing costs, delays, and risks, and increasing freedom, choice, and opportunity.

o Collaboration and innovation: Blockchain and cryptocurrency have the potential and the possibility, to create and generate, collaboration and innovation, for the society, in the mainstream and the society, by fostering and facilitating, communication and interaction, among the users and the investors, as well as the developers and the entrepreneurs, who use and own, the blockchain and cryptocurrency technology and ecosystem, for various purposes and functions, such as buying, selling, or trading goods and services, online or offline, investing, saving, or donating money, online or offline, creating and executing smart contracts, or decentralized applications, online or offline, and more, who can share and exchange, ideas and insights, feedback and suggestions, problems and solutions, on the blockchain and cryptocurrency technology and ecosystem, to create and develop, various platforms and applications, that use and offer, various services and solutions, based on the blockchain and cryptocurrency technology and ecosystem, for various sectors and domains, such as finance, business, governance, and society.

○ **Education and awareness:** Blockchain and cryptocurrency have the potential and the possibility, to create and generate, education and awareness, for the society, in the mainstream and the society, by providing and enhancing, the knowledge and the skills, of the users and the investors, as well as the developers and the researchers, who use and own, the blockchain and cryptocurrency technology and ecosystem, about the features and the benefits, as well as the challenges and the limitations, of the blockchain and cryptocurrency technology and ecosystem, as well as the compatibility and the interoperability, of the blockchain and cryptocurrency technology and ecosystem, with the existing and the emerging, systems and platforms, that are not based on blockchain and cryptocurrency technology, in the mainstream and the society, to ensure and enhance, the functionality and the performance, as well as the adoption and the integration, of the blockchain and cryptocurrency technology and ecosystem, in the mainstream and the society.

- **Economy:** Blockchain and cryptocurrency have the potential and the possibility, to create and generate, various impacts and implications, for the economy, in the mainstream and the society, such as:

  - **Efficiency and transparency:** Blockchain and cryptocurrency have the potential and the possibility, to create and generate, efficiency and transparency, for the economy, in the mainstream and the society, by reducing and eliminating, the friction and the inefficiency, of the existing and the emerging, systems and platforms, that govern and regulate, the technology, the finance, and the society, such as intermediaries, such as banks, brokers, or agents, who charge high fees, cause delays, and pose risks, for the creation and exchange of value, data, and information, on the blockchain and cryptocurrency technology and ecosystem, by using blockchain technology, to create and update a system of records, or a ledger, that is shared and maintained, by a network of users, who collectively manage and maintain, the blockchain and cryptocurrency technology and ecosystem, without the need for intermediaries, such as banks, brokers, or agents, reducing costs, delays, and risks, and increasing speed, accuracy, and accountability.

o Innovation and disruption: Blockchain and cryptocurrency have the potential and the possibility, to create and generate, innovation and disruption, for the economy, in the mainstream and the society, by creating and offering, various types of services and solutions, based on the blockchain and cryptocurrency technology and ecosystem, for various sectors and domains, such as finance, business, governance, and society, that can challenge and transform, the existing and the emerging, systems and platforms, that govern and regulate, the technology, the finance, and the society, such as DeFi, or Decentralized Finance, that aims to create and offer, various types of financial services and products, such as lending, borrowing, saving, investing, trading, and more, using blockchain and cryptocurrency technology, and smart contracts, and decentralized applications, or dapps, that run on various blockchain and cryptocurrency platforms, such as Ethereum, Binance Smart Chain, Solana, and more, that can offer and provide, various types of services and solutions, for various sectors and domains, such as finance, business, governance, and society, that can compete and replace, the traditional and the centralized, systems and platforms, that govern and regulate, the technology, the finance, and the society, such as banks, financial institutions, or corporations, who have high barriers, low accessibility, and limited innovation, for the creation and exchange of value, data, and information, on the blockchain and cryptocurrency technology and ecosystem.

○ **Growth and wealth:** Blockchain and cryptocurrency have the potential and the possibility, to create and generate, growth and wealth, for the economy, in the mainstream and the society, by creating and increasing, the value and the demand, of the blockchain and cryptocurrency technology and ecosystem, as well as the coins, or the digital assets, that run on it, for the users and the investors, who use and own, the blockchain and cryptocurrency technology and ecosystem, for various purposes and functions, such as buying, selling, or trading goods and services, online or offline, investing, saving, or donating money, online or offline, creating and executing smart contracts, or decentralized applications, online or offline, and more, who can benefit and profit, from the blockchain and cryptocurrency technology and ecosystem, by using and leveraging, the features and the benefits, of the blockchain and cryptocurrency technology and ecosystem, such as decentralization, security, anonymity, speed, and more, to create and exchange value, data, and information, in a peer-to-peer way, without the need for intermediaries, such as banks, brokers, or agents, reducing costs, delays, and risks, and increasing freedom, choice, and opportunity.

- **Environment:** Blockchain and cryptocurrency have the potential and the possibility, to create and generate, various impacts and implications, for the environment, in the mainstream and the society, such as:

  - **Energy consumption and emission:** Blockchain and cryptocurrency have the potential and the possibility, to create and generate, energy consumption and emission, for the environment, in the mainstream and the society, by using and consuming, a lot of energy and resources, to run and operate, the network and the blockchain, that supports and maintains, the blockchain and cryptocurrency technology and ecosystem, especially by the nodes, who use a consensus mechanism, called proof-of-work, to create and add, new blocks, to the blockchain, and to verify and confirm, the transactions, events, or actions, on the blockchain. Energy consumption and emission is a trade-off and a balance, between the security and the efficiency, of the blockchain and cryptocurrency technology and ecosystem, as reducing the energy consumption and emission, may compromise the security, and vice versa. Energy consumption and emission is also a challenge and an opportunity, for the blockchain and cryptocurrency technology and ecosystem, to find and adopt, alternative and renewable, sources and methods, of energy and resources, to run and operate, the network and the blockchain, that supports and maintains, the blockchain and cryptocurrency technology and ecosystem, such as solar, wind, or hydro, power and energy, that can reduce and minimize, the environmental impact and footprint, of the blockchain and cryptocurrency technology and ecosystem.

- **Sustainability and responsibility:** Blockchain and cryptocurrency have the potential and the possibility, to create and generate, sustainability and responsibility, for the environment, in the mainstream and the society, by using and promoting, various types of services and solutions, based on the blockchain and cryptocurrency technology and ecosystem, for various sectors and domains, such as finance, business, governance, and society, that can support and enhance, the environmental goals and values, of the mainstream and the society, such as carbon reduction, waste management, or biodiversity conservation, on the blockchain and cryptocurrency technology and ecosystem. Sustainability and responsibility is a requirement and a goal, for the blockchain and cryptocurrency technology and ecosystem, to achieve and realize, its full potential and value, as a universal and versatile, technology, that can offer and provide, various types of services and solutions, for various sectors and domains, such as finance, business, governance, and society, that can benefit and improve, the environment, in the mainstream and the society. Some of the main platforms and applications, of sustainability and responsibility, are:

- **CarbonX:** CarbonX is a platform and an application, of sustainability and responsibility, that are based on the blockchain and cryptocurrency technology and ecosystem, that aim to create and offer, a carbon credit market, or a market, that allows the users, to buy, sell, or trade, carbon credits, or tokens, or digital assets, that represent and certify, the reduction or the offset, of greenhouse gas emissions, or emissions, that contribute and cause, the global warming and the climate change, on the blockchain and cryptocurrency technology and ecosystem. CarbonX is a platform and an application, that use blockchain technology, to create and update a system of records, or a ledger, that is shared and maintained, by a network of users, who collectively manage and maintain, the carbon credit market, and the carbon credits, on the blockchain and cryptocurrency technology and ecosystem, without the need for intermediaries, such as governments, corporations, or agencies, reducing costs, delays, and risks, and increasing transparency, accountability, and impact.

○ **RecycleGO:** RecycleGO is a platform and an application, of sustainability and responsibility, that are based on the blockchain and cryptocurrency technology and ecosystem, that aim to create and offer, a waste management system, or a system, that allows the users, to track and trace, the lifecycle and the journey, of the waste, or the materials, that are discarded or disposed, by the users, on the blockchain and cryptocurrency technology and ecosystem. RecycleGO is a platform and an application, that use blockchain technology, to create and update a system of records, or a ledger, that is shared and maintained, by a network of users, who collectively manage and maintain, the waste management system, and the waste, on the blockchain and cryptocurrency technology and ecosystem, without the need for intermediaries, such as governments, corporations, or agencies, reducing costs, delays, and risks, and increasing efficiency, quality, and sustainability.

○ **BiodiversityCoin:** BiodiversityCoin is a platform and an application, of sustainability and responsibility, that are based on the blockchain and cryptocurrency technology and ecosystem, that aim to create and offer, a biodiversity conservation system, or a system, that allows the users, to support and reward, the conservation and the protection, of the biodiversity, or the variety and the diversity, of the life, on the planet, on the blockchain and cryptocurrency technology and ecosystem. BiodiversityCoin is a platform and an application, that use blockchain technology, to create and update a system of records, or a ledger, that is shared and maintained, by a network of users, who collectively manage and maintain, the biodiversity conservation system, and the biodiversity, on the blockchain and cryptocurrency technology and ecosystem, without the need for intermediaries, such as governments, corporations, or agencies, reducing costs, delays, and risks, and increasing awareness, participation, and responsibility.

What are the Emerging and Innovative Use Cases and Opportunities of Blockchain and Cryptocurrency?

Blockchain and cryptocurrency are not static or stagnant technologies, but rather dynamic and adaptive technologies, that are constantly creating and offering, various types of services and solutions, based on the blockchain and cryptocurrency technology and ecosystem, for various sectors and domains, such as finance, business, governance, and society, that are emerging and innovative, in the blockchain and cryptocurrency ecosystem, and that have the potential and the possibility, to create and generate, various impacts and implications, for the technology, the finance, and the society, in the mainstream and the society. Some of the emerging and innovative use cases and opportunities of blockchain and cryptocurrency are:

- **DAOs:** DAOs, or Decentralized Autonomous Organizations, are a type of platform and application, of blockchain and cryptocurrency technology and ecosystem, that aim to create and offer, a new and alternative, way of organizing and governing, various types of entities and activities, such as businesses, communities, or projects, on the blockchain and cryptocurrency technology and ecosystem, using smart contracts, and decentralized applications, or dapps, that run on various blockchain and cryptocurrency platforms, such as Ethereum, Binance Smart Chain, Solana, and more. DAOs are platforms and applications, that use blockchain technology, to create and update a system of rules, or a code, that is shared and maintained, by a network of users, who collectively manage and maintain, the DAOs, and the entities and activities, that run on it, without the need for intermediaries, such as governments, corporations, or agencies, reducing costs, delays, and risks, and increasing autonomy, democracy, and innovation.

- **Metaverse:** Metaverse, or the Metaverse, is a type of platform and application, of blockchain and cryptocurrency technology and ecosystem, that aim to create and offer, a virtual and immersive, world and reality, that can be accessed and experienced, by the users, using various devices and technologies, such as computers, smartphones, or virtual reality, or VR, on the blockchain and cryptocurrency technology and ecosystem, using various platforms and applications, such as Decentraland, Sandbox, or CryptoVoxels, that run on various blockchain and cryptocurrency platforms, such as Ethereum, Binance Smart Chain, Solana, and more. Metaverse is a platform and application, that use blockchain technology, to create and update a system of records, or a ledger, that is shared and maintained, by a network of users, who collectively manage and maintain, the Metaverse, and the world and reality, that run on it, without the need for intermediaries, such as governments, corporations, or agencies, reducing costs, delays, and risks, and increasing creativity, expression, and fun.

- **Web3:** Web3, or Web 3.0, is a type of platform and application, of blockchain and cryptocurrency technology and ecosystem, that aim to create and offer, a new and improved, version and vision, of the internet and the web, that can be accessed and used, by the users, using various devices and technologies, such as computers, smartphones, or browsers, on the blockchain and cryptocurrency technology and ecosystem, using various platforms and applications, such as IPFS, Filecoin, or Brave, that run on various blockchain and cryptocurrency platforms, such as Ethereum, Binance Smart Chain, Solana, and more. Web3 is a platform and application, that use blockchain technology, to create and update a system of records, or a ledger, that is shared and maintained, by a network of users, who collectively manage and maintain, the Web3, and the internet and the web, that run on it, without the need for intermediaries, such as governments, corporations, or agencies, reducing costs, delays, and risks, and increasing decentralization, security, and privacy.

What are the Risks and Challenges of Blockchain and Cryptocurrency for Security, Privacy, and Regulation?

Blockchain and cryptocurrency are not perfect or flawless technologies, but rather developing and evolving technologies, that are constantly facing and encountering, various risks and challenges, for the security, the privacy, and the regulation, of the technology, the finance, and the society, in the mainstream and the society. Some of the risks and challenges of blockchain and cryptocurrency are:

- **Security:** Security is a risk and a challenge, that affects and influences, the ability and the capacity, of the blockchain and cryptocurrency technology and ecosystem, to protect and safeguard, the transactions and the coins, from cyberattacks, hacks, thefts, and frauds, that can compromise the integrity, availability, and confidentiality, of the data and the assets, on the network, or outside the network. Security is a risk and a challenge, that is affected and influenced, by various factors and events, such as technical issues, human errors, malicious actors, and market manipulations, that can exploit and expose, the vulnerabilities and the weaknesses, of the blockchain and cryptocurrency technology and ecosystem, as well as the users and the investors, who use and own it. Security is a requirement and a goal, for the blockchain and cryptocurrency technology and ecosystem, to find and adopt, various tools and techniques, such as encryption, hashing, digital signatures, multi-factor authentication, and more, to secure and safeguard, the transactions and the coins, on the network, or outside the network.

- **Privacy:** Privacy is a risk and a challenge that affects and influences the ability and the capacity of the blockchain and cryptocurrency technology and ecosystem, to respect and protect the personal and sensitive information and activities, of the users, on the network, or outside the network. Privacy is a risk and a challenge, that is affected and influenced, by various factors and events, such as regulatory actions, legal disputes, social norms, and ethical values, that can demand and require, the disclosure and the exposure, of the information and the activities, of the users, on the network, or outside the network, for various purposes and reasons, such as taxation, compliance, investigation, or identification. Privacy is a requirement and a goal, for the blockchain and cryptocurrency technology and ecosystem, to find and adopt, various tools and techniques, such as encryption, hashing, digital signatures, zero-knowledge proofs, and more, to respect and protect, the information and the activities, of the users, on the network, or outside the network.

- **Regulation:** Regulation is a risk and a challenge, that affects and influences, the ability and the capacity, of the blockchain and cryptocurrency technology and ecosystem, to comply and conform, with the laws, norms, and values, of the existing and the emerging, systems and institutions, that govern and regulate, the technology, the finance, and the society, in the mainstream and the society. Regulation is a risk and a challenge, that is affected and influenced, by the uncertainty and the ambiguity, of the status and the nature, of the blockchain and cryptocurrency technology and ecosystem, as well as the complexity and the diversity, of the transactions, events, or actions, and the coins, or the digital assets, that occur and exist, on the blockchain and cryptocurrency technology and ecosystem, in terms of their legality, their ethics, and their impact, on the technology, the finance, and the society. Regulation is a challenge and a balance, for the blockchain and cryptocurrency technology and ecosystem, to achieve and maintain, its innovation and its disruption, as well as its integration and its acceptance, in the mainstream and the society.

What are the Best Practices and Recommendations for Blockchain and Cryptocurrency Users, Investors, and Developers?

Blockchain and cryptocurrency require and demand, various best practices and recommendations, for the users, the investors, and the developers, who use and own, the blockchain and cryptocurrency technology and ecosystem, to ensure and enhance, the functionality and the performance, as well as the adoption and the integration, of the blockchain and cryptocurrency technology and ecosystem, in the mainstream and the society. Some of the best practices and recommendations for blockchain and cryptocurrency users, investors, and developers are:

- **Users:** Users are the individuals or entities, who use and own, the blockchain and cryptocurrency technology and ecosystem, to create and exchange value, data, and information, for various purposes and functions, such as buying, selling, or trading goods and services, online or offline, investing, saving, or donating money, online or offline, creating and executing smart contracts, or decentralized applications, online or offline, and more. Some of the best practices and recommendations for blockchain and cryptocurrency users are:

- o **Educate and inform yourself:** Educate and inform yourself, about the features and the benefits, as well as the challenges and the limitations, of the blockchain and cryptocurrency technology and ecosystem, as well as the compatibility and the interoperability, of the blockchain and cryptocurrency technology and ecosystem, with the existing and the emerging, systems and platforms, that are not based on blockchain and cryptocurrency technology, in the mainstream and the society, to ensure and enhance, the functionality and the performance, as well as the adoption and the integration, of the blockchain and cryptocurrency technology and ecosystem, in the mainstream and the society.

- o **Choose and use wisely:** Choose and use wisely, the platforms and the applications, that use and offer, various services and solutions, based on the blockchain and cryptocurrency technology and ecosystem, for various sectors and domains, such as finance, business, governance, and society, that suit and match, your needs and preferences, your goals and objectives, your risks and rewards, on the blockchain and cryptocurrency technology and ecosystem, and that are reliable and trustworthy, secure and safe, transparent and accountable, on the blockchain and cryptocurrency technology and ecosystem.

o **Protect and secure your assets:** Protect and secure your assets, such as your transactions and your coins, on the blockchain and cryptocurrency technology and ecosystem, from cyberattacks, hacks, thefts, and frauds, that can compromise the integrity, availability, and confidentiality, of your data and your assets, on the network, or outside the network, by using and applying, various tools and techniques, such as encryption, hashing, digital signatures, multi-factor authentication, and more, to secure and safeguard, your transactions and your coins, on the network, or outside the network.

- **Investors:** Investors are the individuals or entities, who use and own, the blockchain and cryptocurrency technology and ecosystem, to invest and profit, from the blockchain and cryptocurrency technology and ecosystem, as well as the coins, or the digital assets, that run on it, for various purposes and functions, such as buying, selling, or trading goods and services, online or offline, investing, saving, or donating money, online or offline, creating and executing smart contracts, or decentralized applications, online or offline, and more. Some of the best practices and recommendations for blockchain and cryptocurrency investors are:

- **Research and analyze:** Research and analyze, the blockchain and cryptocurrency technology and ecosystem, as well as the coins, or the digital assets, that run on it, in terms of their features and benefits, as well as their challenges and limitations, their design and architecture, their functionality and performance, their value and demand, their history and future, on the blockchain and cryptocurrency technology and ecosystem, to make informed and rational, decisions and actions, on the blockchain and cryptocurrency technology and ecosystem.

- ○ **Diversify and balance:** Diversify and balance, your portfolio and your strategy, on the blockchain and cryptocurrency technology and ecosystem, by investing and profiting, from various types and categories, of coins, or digital assets, that run on various types and categories, of platforms and applications, that use and offer, various types and categories, of services and solutions, based on the blockchain and cryptocurrency technology and ecosystem, for various sectors and domains, such as finance, business, governance, and society, that can reduce and minimize, your risks and losses, and increase and maximize, your rewards and gains, on the blockchain and cryptocurrency technology and ecosystem.

o **Manage and monitor:** Manage and monitor, your investments and your profits, on the blockchain and cryptocurrency technology and ecosystem, by using and applying, various tools and techniques, such as wallets, exchanges, or trackers, that allow you to store and manage, your coins, or digital assets, on the blockchain and cryptocurrency technology and ecosystem, as well as to buy, sell, or trade, your coins, or digital assets, on the blockchain and cryptocurrency technology and ecosystem, as well as to track and trace, the price and the performance, of your coins, or digital assets, on the blockchain and cryptocurrency technology and ecosystem.

- **Developers:** Developers are the individuals or entities, who create and develop various platforms and applications, that use and offer various services and solutions, based on the blockchain and cryptocurrency technology and ecosystem, for various sectors and domains, such as finance, business, governance, and society. Some of the best practices and recommendations for blockchain and cryptocurrency developers are:

  - **Learn and improve:** Learn and improve, your knowledge and your skills, on the blockchain and cryptocurrency technology and ecosystem, as well as the platforms and the applications, that use and offer, various services and solutions, based on the blockchain and cryptocurrency technology and ecosystem, for various sectors and domains, such as finance, business, governance, and society, by using and accessing, various resources and materials, such as books, articles, courses, or tutorials, that are available and accessible, on the internet, or offline, to ensure and enhance, your competence and your confidence, on the blockchain and cryptocurrency technology and ecosystem.

○ **Create and innovate:** Create and innovate, various platforms and applications, that use and offer, various services and solutions, based on the blockchain and cryptocurrency technology and ecosystem, for various sectors and domains, such as finance, business, governance, and society, by using and applying, various tools and techniques, such as programming languages, frameworks, or libraries, that are compatible and interoperable, with the blockchain and cryptocurrency technology and ecosystem, as well as the existing and the emerging, systems and platforms, that are not based on blockchain and cryptocurrency technology, in the mainstream and the society, to ensure and enhance, the functionality and performance, as well as the adoption and the integration, of the blockchain and cryptocurrency technology and ecosystem.

In this chapter, you learned about the potential impacts and implications of blockchain and cryptocurrency for society, economy, and environment, such as financial inclusion, digital sovereignty, and carbon footprint. You also learned about the emerging and innovative use cases and opportunities of blockchain and cryptocurrency, such as identity, voting, and healthcare. You also learned about the risks and challenges of blockchain and cryptocurrency for security, privacy, and regulation, such as hacking, fraud, and compliance. You also learned about the best practices and recommendations for blockchain and cryptocurrency users, investors, and developers, such as education, diversification, and collaboration.

Conclusion

Blockchain and cryptocurrency are two of the most revolutionary and disruptive technologies, that have emerged and evolved, in the 21st century, that have the potential and the possibility, to create and generate, various impacts and implications, for the technology, the finance, and the society, in the mainstream and the society.

In this book, we have explored and discussed, the blockchain and cryptocurrency technology and ecosystem, such as what are the origins and the history, of blockchain and cryptocurrency, what are the concepts and the principles, of blockchain and cryptocurrency, what are the types and the categories, of blockchain and cryptocurrency, what are the capabilities and the functionalities, of blockchain and cryptocurrency, what are the impacts and the implications, of blockchain and cryptocurrency, for the society, the economy, and the environment, what are the use cases and the opportunities, of blockchain and cryptocurrency, what are the risks and the challenges, of blockchain and cryptocurrency, for the security, the privacy, and the regulation, and what are the best practices and the recommendations, for blockchain and cryptocurrency users, investors, and developers.

We have also learned and understood, the features and the benefits, as well as the challenges and the limitations, of the blockchain and cryptocurrency technology and ecosystem, as well as the compatibility and the interoperability, of the blockchain and cryptocurrency technology and ecosystem, with the existing and the emerging, systems and platforms, that are not based on blockchain and cryptocurrency technology, in the mainstream and the society.

We hope that this book has provided and enhanced, your knowledge and your skills, on the blockchain and cryptocurrency technology and ecosystem, as well as your interest and your excitement, on the blockchain and cryptocurrency technology and ecosystem, and that you will use and apply, what you have learned and understood, from this book, to your own purposes and functions, goals and objectives, risks and rewards, on the blockchain and cryptocurrency technology and ecosystem.

Blockchain and cryptocurrency are not static or stagnant technologies, but rather dynamic and adaptive technologies that are constantly evolving and changing, in response to various factors and events, that affect and influence, the technology, the finance, and the society, in the mainstream and the society. Therefore, we encourage and invite you, to keep learning and improving, your knowledge and your skills, on the blockchain and cryptocurrency technology and ecosystem, as well as to keep creating and innovating, various platforms and applications, that use and offer, various services and solutions, based on the blockchain and cryptocurrency technology and ecosystem, for various sectors and domains, such as finance, business, governance, and society.

Blockchain and cryptocurrency are not only technologies, but also visions and movements, that aim to create and offer, a new and alternative, way of creating and exchanging value, data, and information, in a peer-to-peer way, without the need for intermediaries, such as banks, brokers, or agents, reducing costs, delays, and risks, and increasing freedom, choice, and opportunity, for the users and the investors, as well as the developers and the entrepreneurs, who use and own, the blockchain and cryptocurrency technology and ecosystem, for various purposes and functions, such as buying, selling, or trading goods and services, online or offline, investing, saving, or donating money, online or offline, creating and executing smart contracts, or decentralized applications, online or offline, and more.

Blockchain and cryptocurrency are the future of technology, finance, and society, and we are the pioneers and the leaders of the blockchain and cryptocurrency technology and ecosystem. Let us embrace and celebrate the blockchain and cryptocurrency technology and ecosystem, and let us shape and transform, the technology, the finance, and the society, in the mainstream and the society, with the blockchain and cryptocurrency technology and ecosystem.

Acknowledgment

I would like to express my sincere gratitude and appreciation to all the people who have contributed to the creation and completion of this book. Without their support and guidance, this book would not have been possible.

First and foremost, I would also like to thank my family, friends, and colleagues, for their constant love, support, and inspiration. They have been my motivation and my strength, and they have shared with me their insights and experiences in options trading.

I would like to thank Bing, who assisted me in the creation of my book. Bing was a reliable, helpful, and friendly source of information and inspiration.

Last but not least, I would like to thank you the reader, for choosing this book and for joining me to explore the world of blockchain technology. I hope that this book will provide you with a solid foundation and a valuable guide on blockchain technology.

I hope you found my service helpful and valuable. I would love to hear your honest feedback and ratings, as they will help me improve my service quality and customer satisfaction. Please let me know if you have any suggestions or comments on how I can serve you better.

Roman Preciado